Under the
Shadow of *God's*
Wings

This book was inspired by seeing the world through painful years, with yearnings and healings that only God can give. I also sought for eternal comfort by learning how to hear from God and seeking first His ways through the Holy Ghost. Psalm 91 resonated in my soul, strengthening the core for these poems. Read Psalm 91 and you too will understand the mercies of God.

Under the Shadow of God's Wings

DEBORAH HARRIS

Library of Congress Control Number:		2019910676
ISBN:	Hardcover	978-1-7960-4878-0
	Softcover	978-1-7960-4877-3
	eBook	978-1-7960-4876-6

Print information available on the last page.

Rev. date: 07/26/2019

To order additional copies of this book, contact:
Xlibris
1-888-795-4274
www.Xlibris.com
Orders@Xlibris.com
788803

CONTENTS

Through the eyes of God, I love you more than you can imagine. Kiss me with the kisses of your strength. Lead me through the mistful blue of time in the eyes of God. Look to the hill of divine guidance, my love. I'm yours with every beat of my heart.

My Appreciation

When the Lord placed it on my heart to write these poems, I would like to acknowledge God for all His blessings, wisdom, knowledge, and the friends I met along the way: my dear friend Anthony Proctor, who supported me when I needed motivation to touch up finishing points; and my darling friend Nicole Muraoka, who encouraged me even when I wanted to throw in the towel. Thanks be to God for having these friends in my life to go to. Thank You, O mighty God!

LOVE SMILE

Did you not look into my eyes?
What did you see? Did you not
feel my heart beating when we
were close together? Did you not
taste the kisses
of my love?

Let me tell you what you saw:
the smile of love! You are my
rainbow, the
color of blue, comforting in
holding you.
You are my color so bright,
holding me through the night.

You are the one God sent to me
to make me lowly and free.

The meekness you saw in my
eyes to continue,
to strive, to love forever
as long as God commands.

What You Mean to Me

Do you really know or understand
what I demand? You are my father,
the one
to show the way to God down
life's road.
You are my mother, giving
life that's due, letting me
living your dreams come true.

You are my sister so sweet
to protect from harm wherever
you go.
You are my brother to play with
when there's no one around
to bond with.

We are to walk together in the
sunshine, free to
fly wherever we may be, having no
sense of time or dismay.

Many have desire to be
like us, free as the breeze to grow
according to God's will forevermore.

Be Found Still Loving Me

Search for days the wealth of the
earth high and low. Look far and
wide to the end of time, but just
make
sure your love is mine.

Only you can see how precious
you are to me; only they can
guess what it may be. Only you
and I can tell the
story of God best.

Be found still loving me
when things are right
or wrong. Still or not, still
be loving me.

I'll always thank God for you
in the misty blue days. When
things around us seem to stray,
I'll always love you.
Come what may.

DEEP WITHIN MY HEART YOU'LL STAY

Come with me to the waters so
deep, and soon you'll see the
creatures below. How at peace
they seem to be in
low destiny. They go according
to the flow. Only God
knows how they stay that way.

For deep within my heart you
stay, never to decay or stray.
Just like the ocean
so blue, I'm with you. Deep
down in my heart I demand
peace, love, and happiness so
true from you. So in my heart
you'll always stay.

My Raindrop I've Found in You

IF YOU ARE TO WONDER WHAT
I'M SAYING TO YOU ABOUT THE
IMPORTANCE OF THE RAIN,

TAKE YOUR TIME AND LISTEN
TO THE CHIME
THAT RINGS SO SOFTLY IN MY
EAR, SO NEAR,
SO TRUE.

YOU'LL SEE MY RAINDROP
IN YOU.

I DO NOT NEED
BUT ONE EACH DAY TO KEEP
ME ALIVE AS WE PLAY

THE ROLE OF LOVE THAT HAS
BEEN COMMANDED . . .

JUST THE WAY OUR GOD HAS
PLANNED
FOR YOU TO NOURISH ME
EVERY SO OFTEN.
WHY NOT BE MY DOLPHIN

TO PLAY WITH IN THE WATER
OF LIFE, IN YOUR PLACE,
SMILING AT ME IN YOUR PLACE.
SMILING AT ME . . . IN PACE IN
PACE.

YES, YOU ARE MY RAINDROP
I'VE FOUND IN
YOU, SO TRUE. FOR YOU CAME
DOWN FROM HEAVEN
ABOVE TO THE EARTH FOR ME
AND
ONLY ME, MY DEAR. FOR GOD
SAID IT SO. DON'T GO AWAY,
MY LOVE.

KISS ME, I FEEL THE NEED

Do you really know that I
love you? Can't you see? Loving
you as soft as the breeze
that blows in my hair.
Never despair of lost
thoughts unknown. Look
to Jesus. He's always there,
here and everywhere, to
lead you to the light—the
immortal light that
shines forevermore.

Kiss me, I feel the need. Make
known you are with me in those
days.

Love Is a Serious Thing

PEOPLE
LOOK AND WONDER
WHICH WAY TO GO,
ALWAYS SEEKING
FOR SOMETHING
THEY DO NOT KNOW . . .

WHAT IS IT
THAT THEY SEEK?
LOVE
IS WHAT LIFE IS ALL ABOUT,
BEING ABLE TO TRAVEL
THROUGH THE MISTFUL BLUE.

SURVIVAL
IS THE NAME OF THE GAME.
NEVER EVER
BE ASHAMED.
YES, LOVE.
WE ABIDE BY IT,
WE DREAM OF IT,
WE ARE IT.

SO
ALWAYS REACH AND SEARCH
FOR THIS LOVE THAT
COME FROM ABOVE.

Silent Streams

One thing I must say to
you that can be spoken only
through touch, look, and soft
speaking: you are my love, my
love so true.

Do I have to speak the words
to you? Do I have to convince
you? Come closer to my heart.
You'll hear me say "I love you,
my dear."
Be not dismayed no matter
what they may say. God is here
to keep me strong, and you are
mine forever. Seek peace of
mind for it is all right.
Silent streams running
through me, within me, all
around me, being part of me,
forever still me.

Look at Me from My Windowpane

Look and stare at my inner soul,
and soon you'll know what I'm
all about around you.
You'll seek my mysteries untold.
Your very soul will yearn to
learn of my body still, how you
can be real like me!
I'm your day, your morning star,
the breath you breathe in season.
You need no reasoning
to love the things you do for you
forever. So dear, keep
on seeking for riches untold to
the ends of the world. You'll
know, but I'll be there to care
for you still,
for I'm for real.

Look at me from my
windowpane and remain to
receive wisdom untold so you
may grow to be what I seek in
thee.

Turn over the rock of your
imagination and you'll find the
answer that they all seek
is to be above it all, to know all
that they cannot reach.
Don't be dismayed at what I say,
for I'm with you all the way.

I Love the Way You Hold Me

Some seem to introduce
themselves in ways before.
Some seem to love and adore
the way it's supposed to
be, but I love the way you
hold me.

Hold me close in the safety
zone. Mold me so I can be
born to do the things I ought
for you and for me,
so true.

Let me rest upon your breast
and dream of
dreams untold. Be so lovely,
peaceful, and still, my dear,
so real.

Straight to the core of
the heart, I'll come to bear.
Your soul I'll adore.

I Need You, Can't You See!

No other man can move
or groove me the way you do.
You know how to love me.

Your lips so sweet to my
taste set me on fire in places.
You know how to love me.

Moved by your touch, I
need you so much, filled
with your love from above.
You know how to love me.
Thrill me and fill me with
what I need! Can't you
see I'm in need?
You know how to love me!

My True Love to Thee

My true love, I come to thee
with peace, joy, and happiness
fulfilling me. Knowing for
sure life can be beautiful, for
you are a jewel.

Always keep your heart so
pure. Never let hatred or strife
endure. Fill my eyes with
wonder still, knowing always
that you are for real.

SEND THE LOVE

Sweetheart, I come closer to
you, to comfort you, please,
and hold you forever in my
love. Never let us
depart. Send the love, send it
high, send it low. I'll
see and know that peace
has entered in and doubt of
mind has been. Send the love.

My Love to Thee

Words can't express my love
to thee, O Lamb of God, O Lamb
of God. Your loving-kindness
is so deep, my turtle dove, my
turtle dove.
Come closer to my body still.
Cleanse me, mold me, make me
real. I need your love so
concealed. O Lamb of God, come.

You Know! I Really Do Love You

My mind wonders in deep
thought, thanking
my God for what He has brought:

a true love out of time to be mine,
all mine in these dying times.

People come and people go to
that place they do not know, but
our God's hand is stretched out
still to heal and to reveal His will.

You know I really do love you.
What else can I say today, my
love? Just be
with me always today and
forevermore.

Do You Really Know How Much I Love You?

This question must be sought
over and over in time: Do you
not know that I love you so? Let
the breath I take. When I awake,
I see your face.
When I walk, I hear your
talk, for God has commanded
the course.

This is the answer to the
questions that we all must face—
that love comes from above.
Be still and you will see me grow
like a mountain so strong, ever
standing to the end. Sweetly,
tenderly come, my love, for I wait
for you to come.

What True Love Is to Me

What is the coolness of the wind
instead of the heat against your
face, patience in winning after a
long, drawn-out race?

What is light to a child when
frightened or despaired, darkness
to a thief when no one's there at
home?

When peace is in control instead
of confusion, when truth is
spoken
to your heart so soothing.

When faithfulness stands all
by itself, needing no explaining
or help, when side by side
we walk hand in hand, not
trying to impress or make
demands.

For true love is ever free
to have and to hold in Jesus
and me.

LOVE DOES COME EASY

LOOK AROUND, MY LOVELY ONE,
TO BEHOLD THE THINGS
THAT ARE NOT SHOWN.

SMELL THE BRISKNESS OF THE
BREEZE COMING TO THEE, AND
SOON YOU SHALL SEE

THE LOVE FLOWER GROWING IN
MY HEART SOFTER THAN A ROSE
SWEETNESS . . .

EVER LINGERING ABOVE,
COMING DOWN FROM GOD'S
DOME
TO MAKE US A LOVELY FLOWER
IN THESE HOURS . . .

THE SLEEP OF PEACE . . . MY
LOVE, FOR GOD'S LOVE IS PURE
AND GOOD,
THE WAY HE PLANNED
IT SHOULD.

MOTHER DEAR

Mother dear, I want to say I love
you truly day by day. I may not be
there around,
but my love for you always
abounds. Peace is good; peace is
true. Peace is what
I want just from you. Accept my
plea and be patient with me. Your
daughter loves you; one day you'll
see. And as I
close for just a while, continue
to look up and be proud. Your
daughter loves you, loves you true.
One day in the future, I'll be
there with you.

I Do, You Know

Do you know what time
it is?
Do you not know it's noon?
Time has power over gravity,
and so do you.
Power to make my dreams come
true, power to heal me through
and through,
power to walk along life's
darkest road hand in hand. Only
God knows
I do. You know that I love you
so, always now and forevermore.

GENTLE LOVER

JUST LOOK AT YOURSELF
IN THE MIRROR.
WHAT DO YOU SEE?
A VERY GENTLE PERSON
LOOKING AT ME.

TELL ME WHAT YOU
SENSE AT A GLIMPSE,
AND I WILL TELL YOU
THE TRUTH, BABY.

I LOVE YOU
THROUGH AND
THROUGH.
WHEN YOU BEHOLD YOUR
FACE

IN THE MIRROR . . .
I SEE YOU GENTLY
CHANGING
INTO A ROSE
SO SWEET.

FAITHFULNESS ENDURES

December 5, 1980

Her face shines as the brightness of the morning; her breast is as soft as the clouds of the sky. Joy and gladness are in her dwelling, ever abiding so gently. This is my true to be, for me, with me, forever my love. Look away to far-off lands. In my way they shall not stand against me to keep you far from my love so close. Far beyond the distance, the shore lies. I'm yours to walk with so freely near the beaches to explore unseen beauties enduring.

ROSE OF ROSES

Down the road of grief and
despair where so many people
go, they do
not understand or know the
sweetness that lies within, so
tenderly within.

These souls are precious and so
dear. I wish God was near. Do
you not know that He is
a rose? Our God so true? Let
Him come nearer to you and
appear to you, and you'll smell
the fragrances softly blow,
making your life aglow.

Rose of roses in my heart today,
rose of roses to stay. I'll stay
closer to Him always.
Look beyond the blue,
and you'll see Him with you.

I Look Back in Pure Wonder

Looking over my shoulder in
pure wonder,
seeking to know how I got over
the things so
true, so sure, so near, so far.
Only God knows its true nature
revealed.

My memories are softly fading
away—all thoughts of past
experiences that haunt me,
still me,
ever thrilling me.
Only God can tell how He
brought me.

If I could count the moments in
time of my father's plan
for me always,

I'll overcome the same mentally.
Sweet is the victory, yet it is still
to conquer far, near, even so dear
in my being still. Only God
knows it all.

Soon the Flight

Look how long my being has
waited for that time the sky would
be mine, to go to Him who loves
me so, no longer feeling out of
place in this man's fate, wanting
to belong at last to a class of
overcomers
full of grace. Those running in the
race, conquering defeat
pace by pace. Oh! How I long for
such a task at last!

Let not the view of distance make
you weak on your feet and keep
you from climbing high beyond
this worldly seat. Look not at
things that are not, for God is not
far to lead you through
to the winning pool—to swim in
the ocean of His love. Some have
come this far to turn
to vanity and fame,

to discover shame. Let not your
enemy take your rightful place, to
keep you from seeing Jesus's face.

CONTEMPLATING

Contemplating over thoughts
of the past, thanking my
God at last for all the things
He's taught me, brought me,
instilled in me through the
years. How to trust and obey
when there's
no other way. Sought for grace
to run the race and fasted and
prayed, for there's no other
way to
get to know Him more
each day.

Taking time out of time to
think what made it so. Was
it how the mind grew so small
that attracted Him to me
that day I heard Him say
"You're mine"?

I remember sitting still, so
thrilled of hearing His voice,
of course, in my ear. I looked
around, but He could not be
found—this voice so sweet.
He spoke with authority to
me, even me. I answered
Him in my mind with words
unspoken, "Are You talking to
me?" "Yes,"
He said so faithfully. "I found
you to be in My favor," said
the Savior that day. "Come
seek Me and the mystery of
what I am, the Great I Am." I
was so shaken from within
without wanting to know what
it was all about. I started on
my way that day to seek
no matter what it may be.
To the one that loved me so
that day.

YOU ARE AS FRESH AS THE BREEZE

LOOKING UP TO YOU IN
THE BRIGHTNESS
OF THE MORNING
BREEZE, I SEE YOUR LOVE
FULFILLING ME,
STILL GROWING STRONG
AND SECURE, FOR
OUR GOD ENDURES
FOREVERMORE.

AS LONG AS YOU ARE
HERE, MY DEAR,
I WILL ALWAYS BE SAFE
AND SECURE, FOR YOU
WILL ENDURE,
AS THE SUMMER DRAWS
NEAR AS THE SEASONS BE,
I LOVE YOU . . . CAN
YOU SEE!

ALWAYS SMILE
AS SOFT AS THE BREEZE
AND AS SMOOTH AS THE
AIR BLOWING
THROUGH THE TREES,
FOR GOD IS WITH YOU
AND ME.

BY THE SEA . . . ME!

OUR LOVE TRAVELS TO DISTANT
SHORES TO EXPLORE
THE WONDERS OF IT ALL.

WE ARE MADE TO BE ONE IN
THE SON,

OUR SON OF THE MORNING
DEW, ME AND YOU.

DO YOU NOT KNOW ME? I'M
WITH YOU SO NEAR, MY DEAR,
TO KEEP YOU NEAR ME,
TO HEAL, TO FEEL THE
SOFTNESS
OF MY LOVE.

LOOK AT THE SPARROW SO BUSY,
SO TRUE,
SEARCHING FOR SOMEONE
LIKE YOU.
I AM YOUR SPARROW,
SO HUMBLY IN YOUR CARE.
FEED ME WITH LOVE.
LEAVE ME DO NOT DARE.

My Life

Hello, my life! Did you not see
me as I walked by? Did you not
smell my fragrance
as a flower? I walked so softly
while you were sleeping. I kissed
your lips and made you see
my secrets I have never before
revealed.

Hello, my dream! Wake me as I
slowly drift into deep
ecstasy. Do you not know? I
don't want to wake so soon
before
you go.

Keep me always near your heart,
never ever let us depart,
to wander in worlds unknown
alone.
Hello, my bread! Nourish me
and make me fat with love.
Bring me up to the tree of life
to live forever in the sun!
You are my life, my dream come
true. Stay always near.

LET US LISTEN TO THE RAIN

Open your ears. What do you hear?
The beating of the rain upon my
windowpane. It seeks to enter my
deepest thoughts, my secret thoughts.

Soon I awake like a rose to new birth,
ready to give what I'm worth. Many
things seem to come my way, for I'm a
rose brought up for display.

Yes, let us listen to the rain. It will speak
to you; it will tell you the truth. How
God commanded it to come past the sun
to the earth
to bring us life, eternal life so true.

For the rain is part of you. What could
I do without the rain beating against
my windowpane? I couldn't remain the
same.

LAUGHTER IN LOVE

There are many sounds on this earth—
some high, some low—but
not everything spoken is worthwhile.
For God knows the sounds
that touch the heart, my heart so true.
All I want is to be happily in love alone
and to rejoice in laughter—the laughter
in love.

Power to overcome, power in the Son,
power and might to come to me as can
be. When the saints rejoice, the wicked
moan. When the righteous rejoice,
victory is won in the Son—our Son of
righteousness.
So laugh when you are sad. Laugh when
you are glad—the laughter in love.

REASONING IN THESE SEASONS

When walking down life's road,
looking for Him who loves you so,
soon you'll
understand what God demands
from man—His man.

All He wants for us is to see, feel,
and know He loves us so. Let us
sup together, as He says, "Come
and be fed from My body still, for
I'm for real."

He's done all that He said. "I'm the
living bread that came from above
with love,

to feed you and keep you alive so
that you may not die. But what did
they do to
Me that day? They stripped My
garments away. They
beat Me all night in disgrace."

And yet in this season, I reason
to man to understand our God's
command and to accept the Son
and be born into a
new life reknown. So let our God
talk to you, and you'll see His
reasoning to thee.

SOFTLY BY THE STREAM I HEAR HIS VOICE

SOFTLY HE LEADS ME DOWN TO
THE STREAM WHERE I CAN DREAM

I LIE SWEETLY AT HIS FEET.
HE IS MY LIFE, MY LOVE, MY ALL.
HAVE YOU EVER HEARD HIS VOICE?
IT IS LIKE THE SOUND OF MANY
WATERS
DRAWING YOU SO CLOSELY . . .

LET US GO FOR A SWIM IN THE
OCEAN OF HIS MAJESTY, TO DROWN
IN ECSTASY. WHEN YOU RECOGNIZE
WHAT'S HAPPENING, YOU ARE LOST
IN HIS LOVE FOREVER.

LET YOUR THOUGHTS SEARCH IN
THE DEEP WHERE THERE IS SILENT
PEACE.
SOUND IS NO MORE, ONLY
THROUGH THE DOORS.

LET THE FISHES OF THE SEA SPEAK
TO YOU OF MYSTERIES UNTOLD.
FOR THEY CAN TELL YOU OF GOD'S
LOVE UNFOLD.

HOW HIGH AND HOW LOW
THE TRUTH. EVEN CREATION
UNDERSTANDS
GOD'S COMMAND. WHY NOT MAN?

When the Eagle Flies

Soon, my love, the eagle will fly
With sweet melody in my heart—
Secret thoughts within my soul
Only the little bird will know.

Flying high beyond the sky,
reaching with strong desire to be
free from worry, care. Never to
again see one lonely stare.

Soon the east wind so softly will
blow, in my mind I do not know.
Take me far beyond the blue, where
true love can only soothe.

Only once to look below,
Where loneliness so sadly goes.
Look away, my true love be
In my eyes forever me.

CAROUSEL

As we stand in the center of the place,
hearing the laughter filled with peace, a
child breaks the silence.
Come, come down from the top so smooth.
To learn the things so true, step
upon the base of life to explore, cry, and
fight the fight of fate.

Stand quietly and you'll see through the
casement mysteries, can be. Make a wish
quickly
upon it's spell, and yell the laughter of love.
Each turn reveals how it feels to be
lost in a life so in control of grace.

Stop and you'll hear the different sounds
that would make you wonder how it should
be. You can never be
the same without the carousel
that goes round and around, with no
ending fate that lies between each space.

Visions Unfold

Please don't tell me what
life is all about; don't fill me
with false doubt, how man sees
things, not so running the way
of death that grows.

Hell has enlarged itself as God's Word
states what is man's fate.
He's here today and gone tomorrow,
sinking in such sorrow, waiting for the
day of judgment that can be contempt,
that must come to pass to far spent.

Love, My Dove

Call to me, my little dove
I'll send sweet melodies from above
To carry you through the mistful blue, overcoming through and through
I'll speak so softly in your ears and let all doubts quickly disappear to make
sure of my love that's from our God above

JUST IN TIME

I love you with my heart and soul; only God knows. Do you see how good He is to me for sending you down just in time to be mine? I'll always think of you from the east, west, south, and north, because God is the boss. Love always.

PEACE FROM WITHIN

LOOKING THROUGH MY SOUL'S
WINDOW, I CLEARLY SEE
MYSTERIES UNFOLD
TOO HIGH FOR MY MIND . . . TO
TELL THE TRUTH SINKING IN A
LONELY SHELL

LET NOT MY SPIRIT ROAM
TO UNSEEN CHANNELS OR ZONE
TO BE LOST TO SEAS UNKNOWN
KEEP MY BODY SAFE IN LINE
NEVER TO RECEIVE . . .

DEEP OCEANS OF UNKNOWN
CARE I WILL BARE

My One Love

ONE AND ONE EQUALS TWO.
FOUR AND FOUR EQUALS EIGHT.
YOU AND I ARE EQUAL,
ONE UNDER THE SON.

NEVER LET OUR LOVE DEPART
OUT OF OUR HEARTS.
LET LOVE ABIDE ALWAYS AND
LINGER IN OUR EARS. PLEASE
COME NEAR.
I LOVE YOU. CAN'T YOU SEE I
LOVE YOU,
MY HONEYBEE!

SOFT-SPOKEN

Look at me, my love, deep within
my eyes, within the windows of the soul. Soon
you'll see and behold a love
growing rapidly and true, to
make our love secure.

Words lingering in my heart and
soul. I do not know how
to release the little dove within
me. To run and skip upon the
mountains so steep, that I may
find rest at our Lord's feet. Softly
spoken deep words of
love to you, my honey from
above.

THE UMPIRE OF MY FATE

AS I SAT IN THE MIDST OF SPACE,
I HEARD THE UMPIRE OF FATE SAY,
"YOU ARE SAFE," AS I TOUCHED HOME PLATE.

I STOPPED AND WONDERED AT SUCH GRACE
THAT HAD BEEN BESTOWED UPON ME AT THE PLATE
THAT TIME IN SPACE.

DO YOU NOT KNOW HIS DECISION IS FINAL?
WHATEVER THEY SAY?
THEY MAY OPPOSE HIS DECISION
FOR SOME APPARENT REASON, BUT . . .
THEY CANNOT WIN AT HIS CHAIN
OF DECISION.

I REALIZED AS I WATCHED IN AMAZEMENT THE
AUTHORITY AND POWER IN HIS WORDS,
"YOU HAVE CROSS THE HOME PLATE INTO SAFETY," AS
HE WAVED HIS HANDS AND CLEANED THE SLATE.

DO YOU NOT KNOW GOD IS THE UMPIRE OF OUR FATE?
HIS WORDS ARE FINAL AT THE PLATE.
GET IN HIS FAVOR AND DO YOUR BEST. GOD HAS
PROMISED TO DO THE REST.

REGARDLESS OF HOW THE CALL IS MADE, GOD IS THE
UMPIRE OF YOUR FATE!

Going according to the Course

Romans 8:28

GOING ACCORDING TO THE COURSE,
THANKING GOD, THANKING MY GOD
HOW I HAVE BEEN BROUGHT

TO THE PLACE OF SAFETY,
FROM DESPAIR. WHY SHOULD I CARE?
WHAT IS A DARE?

THE TASK I FACE IN THE PLACE OF
REST

GOD HAS GIVEN HIS BEST FOR ME
TO GUIDE ME THROUGH MY QUEST. I
SEEK THE FULL VICTORY, WHATEVER
IT TAKES.

LORD, YOU ARE MY FATE THROUGH
HATE, AND SORROW I WILL BEAR.

Malachi 4:2   7/4/00 at 3:00 p.m.

HEALING IN HIS WINGS

Come close and step aboard for a journey to explore sights in this flight forevermore.

I'll carry you through the mistful blue, gently holding you, so you need not fear.

I'm your conductor through the destiny of life, soaring both day and night, where no one can fly beyond the sky and where pestilence and arrows abide.

Through the winds, the floods, and the waves, I sit still. I pass by, thrilled to see the mysteries of God's glory revealed. I have no care as I stare to see Satan's seat, so thrilled to know God is in control to command man's fate below that.

As I sit so uniquely upon His wings toward my bright mansion, I lean upon His wings in this flight. The clouds address me, for they know God's plan to take me to Jesus just over the land that awaits me. I'm continuously healing safely on His wings as I comfortlessly abide, never to stride for care around me.

There's still plenty of room on this eagle's wings where I lie, always being healed as I lie still. I've become like one of these! See! Feel the breeze, be healed, stay filled, for I'm for real!

Jesus, Nice of You to Stop By (12-3-01 at 10:45 p.m.)

Hello, Jesus, nice of You to stop by. Don't be a horror to me by showing me Your wound-pierced side. Just reveal to me Your hands and feet; the rest of Your body I want to be deprived. For I know You were the sacrificial lamb for me that day when they stripped Your skin away. Yes, You were a bloody mess, for You gave the ultimate best for us that day (life). When I beheld Your face, I saw no eyes. Did they at the cross that day have no shame to remove them from You too? But I still see flaming eyes of love as bright as the sun piercing my being and making me whole. You did quietly sit at my bedside and held my hand and revealed what I can stand. Truly You are the bread of life—that manna from above. I will forever be whole by discerning what You did for me at Calvary.

WATCH HER, SHE'S A GROUPIE

There are many people who follow the crowd; they say it is to be safe from being out of place in man's fate that's just for a short time in line. I guess when walking alone, you're easily shown that you're really up to par in the eyes of God and man. With the demand to be upright in the fight for righteousness, you'll walk this path alone. To overcome your greatest foe, you'll have to watch as you know the crowd that seems to be so occupied in the stream of despair. They don't care how or where she leads them as long as they are not shown the light that will lead them home. Her voice is enticing and so inviting, causing you to lose your thoughtful view. Have you noticed her style? For a while she arrays herself in perfect play to deceive those trusting in her care. They do not dare seek to know her worth, given on earth, about the secret things revealed in front of God's face on the hill of disgrace, as she plays the harlot in the chalet under her will. She'll make you dream of pleasure, never wanting to sever her will in your body still. Watch her; she's been ordained this way to deceive the chosen few and to make them stray from the way of glory with her beauty on display before your eyes in the cloud of dreams. God has promised her end. Don't fret. Just keep your eyes on the Lord above with love.

THE PRICE

Someone spoke and told me what a great price You paid on Calvary. How God sent You to earth to give us eternal life rebirth. I was confused just like Nicodemus, who asked how we humans can be born again. I needed someone to open my understanding of what God was commanding. You mean I must give up my life, too, to be made anew? No one could have done what You did on that day to save us from decay. Yes, there is an ultimate price we all must pay to receive You today. To seek You, love You, keep Your Word in our hearts so we can depart from below, looking for You at every corner from the people we meet. Look into hungry souls and hear the cries for salvation. This price You paid You become like we so. When we cry, You can come near to heal, save, and make us whole. We really don't know what price You paid on Calvary, but we are glad You did it anyways.

ON THE OTHER SIDE OF REALITY

It was a hard battle just trying to exist in a bliss of time and space. Wondering what it would be like being me, the real me—so new. Someone told me to be myself and to be no one else in order to be as free as I can be! Now I've just begun living in the sun of time and grace—no longer disgraced by living others' fate. On desiring to be like someone else, I discovered a new place where no one has strode in life's path at last. It truly felt good to have room regardless of the doom in the choices that I'd make in the future. Yes, on this new land where God has commanded all of us to tread. How can we be His servants to do His biddings unless we are willing to see oneself face-to-face in the glass of our future, our divine future? We speak to each other about who we want to be instead of seeking to be real. I haven't found many traveling this road, but at last I can. Proverbs 23:7 states, "As a man thinks so is he." So let people see the real you as you paint upon the canvas of life.

YOUR SHOES
(PROVERBS 31 WOMAN)

Do you really know who wants to walk
in your shoes? The constant decisions
you must make daily from your post
through the Holy Ghost?

For God has placed you in these shoes
that surround you with many a care—
you there, here, and everywhere.

For you must smile while others frown;
you must care when others stare. You
must hold up the standard of light
throughout the night while everyone
is sleeping and forces are peeping to
remove us from God's plan.

Praying in season for no apparent
reason in the shoes you must wear in
despair. But God has anointed you for
such a task; you will last.

Your husband adores the steps that you
take, every moment you walk in God's
grace. Your children hear the praises
among
the lilies that grow at your feet.

For you are a woman of wisdom, of
power, and of grace, standing so lovely
in your place.

For God has special rewards for people
like you, people that walk in your shoes,
for only you can at God's command. Be
strong and stomp out doubts and fears,
for Jesus
will hear you when you're near.

Last but not the least, stand your post,
secured and strong, and one day you'll
exchange those shoes for a crown.

THE AWAKENING

Silence is my dwelling in a lonely shell. I cannot tell the sounds that come to mind in time of dreams. Wishing to be free and to think as clear as the breeze, having the change to glance at life's best. But having no strength in length for the task, suddenly before a twinkling of an eye, you sense new birth coming slowly to surf. Soon you're new again, as if you have never been the way you were before. You strive to catch the missing link as you think anew. It's good to be renewed in mind and soul, to behold the beauty of life on both sides, and to swell the scent of care around you. You'll bear with delight in the light of light. His goodness you now can see, not being deceived in the way you felt it should be. Led by man's hand, dense in a sense until the change came, now you are never to be the same again. Climbing new heights to do what's right, to keep the mind in time with the chime of a new dawning. Awake to the strength of knowledge you have been given from above for God's purpose and will. Enjoy this new birth that has sprung into existence at His will.

Empty Soul, Listen

How does it feel when the lights go out
and the cold of darkness sets in? Into
your soul? Someone just spoke to you
about Jesus again, you know.

How does it seem to think of the
distance you placed yourself from
entering into
life where sweet roses of fragrant
life pass over your soul through the
night?

Dreams of peace, love, and joy that
only Jesus Christ can give in the midst
of the coldest winters of your life.

Don't let the word of life pass your
heart again so soon to miss out on what
God wants to do for you.

He paid a great price to give eternal life
to the man He has created for
His glory on earth.

So accept the Son and allow the
sun of righteousness to flow to that
empty hole in your soul. Only
He can fill it with His peace.

Day unto Day I Hear His Voice

Many sounds are heard in the ears of man, but nothing so gentle to the soul that the voice so bold yet precise and quick to the point to lead to the path of life. Let me ever draw nigh to the joyful sound around God's throne. His voice brings life and deliverance over oppression and grief. Soon having relief in a world full of heartache and pain, I'll gain. I will always draw closer to the chains that start this healing voice in my ear again.

THE JOURNEY

As I sat on board in space, I noticed in the face of each passenger in place the look of each one's destiny so sure. I wondered in mind as the plane excelled to forty-five thousand feet who the crew on board this fleet were, whom the commander-in-chief had appointed. Soon the stewardess appeared to take the orders of the day as we went on our way to the land of sunny delight on high. The crew looked secure as the pilot took control of the fleet through the turbulence that kept us up a heap of moments. This made me admire the pilot and helped me rest quietly as I watched the crew's self-control.

HASSLE IN BUSINESS

Let me see, what do I want to purchase today at the store? Things are such a bore. Standing in line, hoping to score the sale of the century (ooh!). My feet hurt; it's so sore. I don't know why we suffer the lore given by the store. Let us break away from their hold on our cash, to be free at last. Let's break the hassle that traps us in the seasons of fuss and lust. There's never enough to fill this hole in the soul from taunted needs. I'm going home. My feet hurt!

Touch Me at Your Risk

Many people think that you are to go in the way of the natural all the time, but let's take our time and think this one out before we get too far out of sorts—in what man has brought to the minds of people that are weak. God never planned that we bend so much to the way it is on this earth. Wake up! For now is the time to seek for the chime that rings so loudly in our ears, saying that man's end is near. We best get close to the Savior and be in His favor on the day He'll take us all away to appear before the judgment seat down at His feet, seeking for full relief to be known at the throne on that day.

What are you willing to give for that day? To see God's face shining brighter than the sun that just begun to shine a minute ago? Touch Him at your risk, and you'll never be the same. Kiss His lips so sweet to remain at His feet, listening to His voice, and you'll agree, as humble as a bee, that the degree is sure. You'll endure to the very end. Touch Him and feel the love flowing through your mind and soul that makes you whole again. Kiss His cheek and taste honey sweeter than the honeycomb. Smell His garments and be protected under the shadow of His wings. Start over again. Touch Him at your risk. Don't be afraid, you'll never be the same again.

Now Is the Time

Now is the time for love—no
matter what time of day. Now
is the time for peace. Don't care
where it may come. Now it is
time for harmony in the soul of
man to calm the raging seas.

Now it is time for
enlightenment—only from God
to see things
as they should be.

Now it is time for dreams—
of future view—for the
Word of God is true
concerning you.
Now it is time!

Footsteps in the Dark

I quickly observe the sharp thing that passes my eyes that can't be disguised. Swiftly they come to destroy your way at the bay of life. Keep your eyes looking straight ahead, lest you will be led astray from the day that surrounds you. There are many people who don't know the difference in a show of footsteps that lead many on their way. Stay in the zone where you are, and in God's time, there is safety, if you may. His arms are there stretched out still to heal.

BEHIND THE EYES OF GOD

Where I behold the earth so low, where corruption
abides and darkness lurks, comes to birth
bringing sickness, darkness, and darkness.
Can you imagine how our
God feels after all that's
been revealed? He gave
His only begotten Son to come.
He showed man the way back to life, but
what do they want from God's secret thought?
He's done everything that's commanded.

Between the Sheets (1/2/08)

The soft winds blew with sweet essence of fragrances from the clothing on the line, freshly washed with tender care, while I stared at how white they were. I was a child who was used to seeing such sight throughout my life when Mom rose early to wash with her might to make sure they were clean. I've been told not to play with the sheets and had been scorned at her feet many times before. But I loved to smell the sweet fragrances of purity that hung lovely, so one day I rebelled and felt a presence among the sheets. I couldn't tell who it might be. Only fear grasped my heart when I heard her voice say, "Come out from the sheets and look at my face." Awe gripped my soul because I felt safe among the sheets instead of her presence. There I could dream of life and fantasize that the world smells this way. The moment I departed the clothesline, my imaginary world, I had to face the discipline that awoke me from beyond the sheets.

CONQUERING TO CONQUER

Strive to enter that pathway that leads to unseen heights of victory never experienced before, and I guarantee you'll seek for this place to be one with the Creator—being in His favor and overcoming man and foe. Let no one tell you that the battles of this life are based on what appears, but what isn't revealed is what takes effect upon our best on the earth, our earth. Many teachers, scholars, and such think they know so much about God's plan for man, His man, for sure. Don't be blind in your mind to seek for what's right about this fight that rages on and on. Stand on the promises of His words that state, "Conquer all gates that you enter in." Conquering to conquer the unseen foe, conquering to conquer forward as we go no matter the task, for our God's will, will last.

Love, My Dove

Call to me, my little dove,
I'll send sweet melodies from above,
To carry you through the mistful blue,
Overcoming through and through.

I'll speak so softly in your ear,
Let all doubts so quickly disappear,
To make you sure of my love,
That's of God from above.

Just in Time

I love you with my heart and soul; only God knows. Do you see how good He is to me for sending you just in time to be mine? I'll always think of you from the east, west, south, even north, because God's the boss. Love always.

CPSIA information can be obtained
at www.ICGtesting.com
Printed in the USA
BVHW071000050819
555096BV00009B/265/P